When I Pick Up My Wings from the Dry Cleaner

By Lisa J. Cihlar

BLUE LIGHT PRESS ◆ 1ST WORLD PUBLISHING

1ST WORLD
PUBLISHING

SAN FRANCISCO ◆ FAIRFIELD ◆ DELHI

Winner of the 2013 Blue Light Poetry Prize

When I Pick Up My Wings from the Dry Cleaner
Copyright ©2014 by Lisa J. Cihlar

1ST WORLD LIBRARY
PO Box 2211
Fairfield, Iowa 52556
www.1stworldpublishing.com

BLUE LIGHT PRESS
www.bluelightpress.com
Email: bluelightpress@aol.com

BOOK & COVER DESIGN
Melanie Gendron

COVER PHOTOGRAPH
Emma N. Coen

AUTHOR PHOTOGRAPH
Karen M. Byerly

FIRST EDITION

ISBN: 978-1-59540-959-1

TABLE OF CONTENTS

A Double Life in Twenty-Nine Days, Twelve Hours, and Forty-Four Minutes

The moon is a golden bellied, pregnant turtle, a flit and a flirt, waxing and waning, living in star squalor. A constellation hoarder. Like the cat lady, so much hair all over her house, it's like living in a cocoon. She has a passing thought, wonders if cats ever get free-floating, towel-clinging, aggravating cat hair in their eyes. Her own are constantly weeping. Today she folds a flock of paper cranes. Tonight the moon magic sets them free to fly across her face. The old man down the road, who wears plaid shirts every day, and pants held up with binder-twine suspenders, ambles his white turkeys down a forest path. Here and here and here are the best places to lay a clutch of almost round eggs. They light the dim corners where jack-in-the-pulpit and trillium choir. The origami frogs and toads are singing in the marsh, squirting their own strings of moon pearls.

Coffee Klatch

When she closes her eyes, the nocturnal katydids in her ears chirrup. The last full moon of winter, a maple sugar moon, illuminates a rabbit huddled beside a shrinking, grainy snowdrift, spills in her bedroom window, wakes her from a nightmare she forgets instantly. Still, a lingering unease sends her out before the sun crests to join farmers drinking coffee at the Iguana Café. Theirs is a silence she can live with. As they leave the restaurant and step onto the macadam, three turn into crows and take wing. The remaining farmer holds his implement cap to shade his eyes and thinks, *It looks like rain.* She hears him.

Gulp

The toad squints from under the trillium in the shade garden. He follows me to my back door and begs his way in. He says he wants to live with me and hunkers down by the cats' water bowls. I'm not sure, but toads can be princes they say, so I scoop him up and tuck him away. He causes one of the kittens to be born deformed and dead. This is a kind of power I never wished for.

We both sit slumped in the lamplight on the flabby green couch and I watch him tongue flies from the window screen and grow more substantial with each gulp. The clowder of seven cats on my bed has turned me nocturnal, so I am up all hours with him. They are the only reason he has not opened his throat and swallowed me down. Still, the bigger he gets, the stronger the reek of dried banana chips. I can't predict what that means, but the cats are restless and twitchy tonight.

When I Pick Up My Wings from the Dry Cleaner

I learn to tie a sheepshank with a rough fiber rope to hold tight. I bring home Chinese carryout with a fortune cookie to advise me what to do next week. For the first time ever, my cookie is empty. Instead I make my atheist prayer: Dear catalpa tree with screaming flower faces, I will collect your sphinx moth caterpillars and make a fishing trip north where tall lodge pines grow and the creeks hold ice late into spring. It is lonely sitting lakeside with an acre of rope. I will tie every knot in *The Ashley Book of Knots*. One of them is sure to hold when I pick up my wings from the dry cleaner.

Blood Rite

Sexing turtles is all about vents and concave and convex. Caves have stalactites and stalagmites. Belly buttons are innies or outies. White towels mean I've grown up. I have sat on a white towel and bled. The smear like tie dye makes me cry. Back to my red-eared slider and wondering if all females bleed? I stand guard over the washing machine at the laundromat protecting my colored panties and red streaked towels from embarrassment. Pour hydrogen peroxide on the stain and watch it bubble. That is the homemaker's tip of the day. When I have a boyfriend, I will go into a tent for one week a month and hide. That is what the women of the Bible did. I will take my turtle with me. She with the high-domed shell packed with eggs.

Moult

Leftover shell of a cicada, translucent amber, attached by hooked feet to a willow leaf. A slit up the back so small I wonder at the conjure it took to seep away. On the screen over the kitchen sink, a watered-down green of empty mayfly still clenches, tail whiskers aquiver in the breeze. A minute desiccated toad on the cool concrete garage floor behind the head of my spade. The skull of some slight animal complete with teeth and wormy line down the center locking both halves together like a puzzle. A tattered spider's web with silk-wrapped prey. Hanging from a milkweed leaf, a monarch chrysalis gone from pale jade to clear with pin studs of gold still garnishing its widest circumference. The eggshell of some small bird, white, chalky, with a loose piece of membrane, brittle now, it sticks to my sweat damp finger until I lose it to the wind. Finally, feathers: red, blue, black and white checked, most an undistinguished mottled brown. A glue gun and me. The broken, headless, one-handed torso of a mannequin hauled home from the dumpster behind Shopko. Using the fragments, I paste together my fresh self. A cachet I never had before. When I return from the hollow in the lightning-struck oak, rotting from the inside out, they ask me why. I consider the answer while combing splinters from my hair.

Spiral

This is the day that pain made. A spiral shelled snail creeping over shattered glass shards from a mayonnaise jar, dropped by a boy child. It spilled ants and sand and twigs across the north-side algae-green walkway that is always slippery and more so in the rain. This is the day that pain made. A spiral shell edging along the blacktop where winter salts, spread by the man, have yet to succumb to spring showers. This is the day that pain made. A spiral inching under emerging spilt milk hosta leaves where the woman sprinkled diatomaceous earth. This is the misty slime trail that pain left.

Tartar Sauce and Salsa

Dreaming of mayonnaise and ketchup, a condiment man sleeps under the house. His first drink is coffee and a splash of brine, stirred with a kosher dill pickle spear to salt it up. His morning begins at midnight when the rest of us are just staggering to bed. He slithers out from under, smearing a gob of prepared horseradish sauce on the foundation where it turns away termites. He has no idea that he is useful in that way. At the all-night corner diner booth, he hunkers alone and demands hot water and five mustard packets. He twirls his spoon 7 clockwise, 11 counterclockwise because he is a prime number guy. The Thai girl he loves is wearing a new yellow slicker when she dances to the tinkle bell above the fingerprint door. She has never been to Thailand, but she carries a bottle of fish sauce from her mother's stash. She has tied a big red bow with 23 ribbon loops around her neck. On the nights when condiment man is unavailable, she joins a drumming circle and plays a djembe with a stretched goatskin head. She is coordinated and extraordinary.

Skunk Stroll

These are the things she buried: the skull of her pet rabbit whose name was Sometimes Fred, a dog whistle, a pair of purple knitting needles, a feather from a guinea hen, all black and white laddered. She climbs the oak and joins herself to the trunk with streamers of spider web, and weary people come to watch her turn to shaggy bark. It is taking a long time, but that she expected. The people send up sandwiches using the pulley system she pilfered from a tree house where the children no longer play. The Ladies Garden Club brings old tires and fills them with dirt to plant Sweet Williams and Purple Viking potatoes. One morning she sees a man walking his white turkeys. In the evenings when all the people have gone back to their domesticities, she watches a family of skunks tumble past in the moonlight. She dreams when it is windy, but mostly about the stove and iron. Did she remember to turn them off?

The Optimist Does Origami

She has faith that flat paper will turn into a crane. That the cranes will return from south wintering to strut the northern greening fields. She believes in yellow. Not only dandelions, but the yellow sky before tornadoes, and the yellow dog named Ned. The dog that leads his master to the best dumpsters every evening in alleys behind grocery stores and fancy restaurants to fill the wooden wagon they pull behind. It is her conviction that better is a state of mind. She trusts that Orion will return and she will stand outside on a frozen lake on the coldest night of the year with the ice cracking like rifle blasts. There will be the star spray. She will point it out to her nephew again and again until he can see it and follow the belt to Sirius. She will tell him it is called the Dog Star and that he can always navigate back to her. He falls sound asleep in the ice shanty where they fish for walleyes, and the propane heater keeps it warm enough to melt the icy globes off his wool mittens. She watches his slumber and folds fortune tellers all night long to hold his dreams.

The Muralist

The self-named Gas Station Slut works the cash register, sells bait and fishing tackle, makes donuts every morning in the big fryer, nine at a time, and cleans chicken parts delivered three times a week by Holstead Meat and Poultry. Cold legs and wings, breasts and thighs, dumped into stainless steel sinks of icy water. She cuts off the thick yellow fat, uses her thumbs to push out bloody red pulp, possible lungs. They are not the heart or gizzard, she knows those parts. They may hold the last breaths of the white chickens filled with farm air; clover and lilac. The warm scent of a cup of milk splashed into a plastic bowl for the feral cats that race in from all corners of the barn where they crouched watching for mice and rats. The Gas Station Slut spends her nights at home painting murals on the walls. She puts a chicken into every one. And rainbows, she is big on rainbows.

Thesaurus Banned

She spent decades researching the perfect words. Brain crabbed fist tight, reading dictionaries, road signs, and medicine bottles. Old friends were supposed to tell her enough is enough. Unfortunately, they had babies to raise up and fields to harrow. It was a boring task anyway, they whispered, in the rooms where some went to breastfeed just to get away. Especially now that they had these perfect babies.

She buys a two-story nook and cranny house and rents the rose papered, sparse, spare bedroom, tucked under the eaves, to an old Vietnamese woman, blue-black hair down to her knee-backs, the one who serves fish sauce as condiment to tourists from a cart on the corner of 4th and Main. Hair stolen from her boar bristle brush spells words in cursive on the cold stone basement floor and the wooden porch beneath the chain swing.

Every poster in the post office lobby is printed in bold, "FBI MOST WANTED"—never the "UNWANTED." The guilty, not the innocent. A Baltimore oriole constructs a basket nest in the ficus tree that she moves outside every spring. The nest is lined with a long dark lock, ruins the sentence. Runes of the sentence.

Small Scale Poultry Keeping

When Mr. died of a stroke and Mrs. died of a broken heart, the white turkeys, rusty chickens, and Muscovy ducks took over the house. The ducks insisted on the attic where they slipped into old smoking jackets and bridesmaids' gowns they found in wooden trunks plastered with mailing labels from around the world. The chickens claimed the bedrooms and laid pale green and brown eggs on the goose-down pillows, and the turkeys, they went wherever they wanted. The television remote was lost before they moved in, so it was public TV all day and white noise after Jack Horkheimer, Star Gazer. Thanks to Sesame Street, the fowl are learning to count. There are 56 eggs in the house, and maybe a few more that one old chicken misplaced. Thanks to The Nature Show, when the red fox from the quarry comes knocking at the door, they know enough not to answer. So far every one of them is ignoring the pigeons on the roof. The pigeons wing into town looking for reinforcements on top of the grain elevator.

Memorial Day

Carp in the river flowing from Yellowstone Lake strung in blurry underwater dashes, facing upstream with mouths wide, waiting for aquatic morsels that jerk along, fighting the current. Ripe strawberry gills flash sideways smiles. They appear and vanish like a magician's three of hearts. Farm boys stand on the grassy banks, slim sun-browned herons, with arrows nocked, strings taut, watching. They know their weapons and their intentions. A cloud pauses the sun's reflection. Smooth opaque mirror turns transparent. Arrows slice silent through the water, through the targets. Tuesday, after the long holiday weekend, the birch and pine woods, pressing against the river, stink of rotting fish. Turkey vultures kettle in the updrafts. Scales spark and crows feast.

Chain-Link

They haul the chain-link fence to the metal man for extra cash. The feral wolfdog that used to crouch and slink behind that fence is gone now, dead or sold, possibly escaped, maybe eaten. A thing you might run into on a dark road in the middle of a moonless night when the fog is rising from the rain-saturated corn fields. A ferocity that skulks down alleys and under houses, terrified and treacherous.

I dream of wild cats—lynx, puma—that vault so high they escape enclosures to stalk suburban backyards among carefully tended roses and patio tomatoes. All parents are fearful and walk their children to the bus-stops. Fanatical men climb zoo fences and plummet in on bears and lions, then look astounded when devoured.

Metal is selling at all time high prices. Thieves scuttle under trucks parked for the night at city garages and rip out catalytic converters for precious metals. One night they meet escaped creatures and howls ensue.

If Your Love has Left You, This Will Break Your Heart

Driving out of the city on Fish Hatchery Road, tall concrete and brick buildings change over to flashing sprinkler duplexes and ranch style houses, then fields of corn and soybeans. Retired red barns, new metal sheds, silos, in upright repair and sinking disrepair, stud the acres. On your left, at the 5-mile mark from the last crossroad is a cattail marsh and shallow broad pond. A minute gravel pull-off.

Before sunset in August, when the water pinkens up, you can see wakes from muskrats swimming toward their evening chewing of sweet stems and roots and the occasional frog or crayfish. Cattail lodges punctuate the water. In the twilight, in silhouette, each mound will be topped by a single Canada goose. Just so.

A Brief Encounter

The wolf at my door asks to use the telephone. Seems the radio collar around his neck won't tune to his favorite Jazz and Blues station anymore. He looks in the yellow pages for the number of a scientist. The coot he carries under his left arm looks worried. There are no scientists listed. Naturalists either. The wolf asks if I have a Phillips screwdriver because, to hell with it, he'll fix it himself. I keep a screwdriver in the garage. Upon my return, the coot looks relieved. The widgeon drake under the wolf's right arm looks alarmed and restless. The wolf sees me staring and comments that the American Widgeon makes excellent table fare. He asks me to hold the duck and mud hen while he stands in front of the bathroom mirror trying to figure out everything backwards. The widgeon, sensing trouble, cries out a flurry of alarm calls. The coot looks worried and tries to put his head under his wing. I hear B.B. King singing in my bath. The acoustics are damn fine in there. I open the front door and send the birds into the bright cerulean. Arms free, I can dance with the wolf.

The Dairy Farmer Told Me His Cows Were Coming into Season

In clouds of chokecherry blossoming spring, the English sparrows flew right into the bluebird boxes and pecked through the skulls of the nestlings. This is a true thing I regret. In the humid mildew of summer, you play Thelonious Monk. It is too loud and I can't think. It might surprise you to know that I don't like that music. I want to, but I regret that I don't. His middle name was Sphere. For that I am grateful. I am happy to see that you have brought home the seagulls to graze the lawn. We must remain respectable or they might send us back to Budapest. I don't like goulash. The dobos torta though, I could eat it every day. The hogshead of wine is delivered in the fall. Turned on its side, the goats like to balance, while the cows watch from the feedlot next door. I saw you dance on it at midnight one full moon ago. I might have joined you, regret that I did not. The man who took me to the ocean was so old, his face was collapsed. But his blues guitar—oh, it was a wonder. I have only seen one ocean, and the trip over the mountains in winter through avalanche country froze my ears. That is why I can no longer hear you. It is something I regret, and I wonder if one ocean is enough. The Danube might as well count. I want you to know that I was packing away the hot weather clothes, and I accidentally put your brother somewhere. Now I can't find him and I regret that I didn't mention it sooner.

Tone Deaf

Mary purchased a Les Paul blues guitar she didn't know how to play. She hung it on the wall over the baby grand piano she didn't know how to play. Whenever she walked past the music room, that used to be her dining room, she would pluck a G-string and stand still until the reverberations stopped. When she dusted the top of the shiny ebony piano, she would hit one note and listen to it fade. She couldn't read music and had no idea what she was playing, even though she knew every good boy does fine. One Saturday she tapped a key on the piano and plucked a string on the guitar at the same time. She danced a single step and flipped her dustrag in the air. When she called the piano tuner and he played part of a suite by Liszt, she never opened the fall again. She took the guitar to Goodwill and on the way home bought two canaries from the dime store and a cage with a bell and a mirror.

It Sure is Dark in Here

Being inside a bear is not like being inside a confessional. Not that I should know, not being Catholic, but on tour in Europe I visited a lot of CRMs—Cathedrals, Ruins, and Museums. I tested out a confessional. It was dim and musty, but nothing close to the dark inside a bear. In the confessional I could smell the spice of incense from the boat swung by a priest, and maybe a hint of sacramental wine. The bear smelled of blueberries and gin, which probably came from the juniper berries that grow here in the north where the soil is sandy and acid. Listen inside the confessional and you will hear the black-robed choir singing Hallelujah. If your confessor is hungry for a parishioner's Sunday supper of fried chicken, mashed potatoes and gravy, with gooseberry pie for dessert, you may hear his stomach gurgle. And the bear's for grubs and wild greens. His heartbeat, slow and deep thumping. It is moist inside a bear and dry in a confessional. There is a bit of velvet in both. Still, no matter what you confess inside a bear, you will find no forgiveness there.

Starlings

A flock from the copse of honey locust on our east acre. A flock from the west, flying over a corn-stubble field, dusty with morning snow. The third wave, gathered and chattering in two maples just north of the house. They come together suddenly, and swing up into maiden blue-eyed sky, slightly off kilter for the count of three. Then muscle momentum memory and they become one, a perfect, living, breathing, pumping machine. A kaleidoscope, a flashing sparkle of glassy obsidian. They somerset and twist over the barn, reverse over the house, off to the south and gone. You are asleep. There is no one else to tell, and I don't have the words to tell it.

Desire Doesn't Work Here

The wolf chewed her heart out. It was in the blackest part of the night when old quilts of much-washed muted scarlets and blues and greens were piled so thick she couldn't move, even to cover her mouth when she yawned or screamed. Sand-colored moths bounce at the window screen again, and she never knew what exactly they wanted. Maybe they desired the woolen skirts in the closet, where their pearly eggs would hatch and minute worms would chew holes right across the black and orange plaid. If she looked long enough at the fabric, held up to the morning light chunking in the window, she could have read the message and known what would happen before it did; that the wolf with shining cold yellow eyes would cross the yard and the threshold and bound up the stairs on silent pads. The sentry dogs didn't even whimper in their heavy pregnant sleep. There was only one way to stop it, and it had to do with the moon and a rabbit, so afraid it could not move from its crouch under the bridal wreath next to the half empty corn crib. If she knew the rest of the spell, she might own empathy.

Donations

We carry our used body parts to St. Vinnies. They have my left foot and leg now. And your kidney along with ten pairs of who-are-you-kidding pants, plus the boxers that might fit, but the pink heart over the crotch is a no go. On the way home from dropping off my two-foot braid, we stop at Dairy Queen and the Dollar Store. The sign in the window says NO FOOD OR DRINK, so we stand outside finishing our turtle sundaes. You tell me our neighbor donated her laugh last week. I say we could probably buy it pretty cheap; it would be nice to have around in the middle of winter. You say, if we're willing to drive to the city, they will have better ones at Goodwill.

These Days I Go by the Name Compass

Magnetic north is now moving from Canada to Siberia at 40 miles per year. Some things are true because they are true and measurable, and some things are only my truth. Pins and Styrofoam and dead bodies in the freezer. Beetles are easy. So are moths and butterflies. Ants are hard due to their size. Silverfish impossible. Anything that begins as a wet body, that smears easily under a hand or shoe, doesn't pin well or hold up if you manage to pin it down, even with an acupuncture needle. Wet bodies dry up, shrivel, and become brittle dust. I make labels. Scientific name, common name, where collected. I have a shelf full of guide books to insect identification. Bird books, too. How many birds have hit the windows? They have magnetite in their skulls. They can find their way home from anywhere. That is a place I have not been in a hundred years. Now that north is moving so fast, the birds may be just as lost. They call me with birdsong that my vocal cords are not prepared or evolved to repeat. I will leave them bright yarn in the pine boughs for building nests and teaching nestlings what to sing for.

About the Author

Lisa J. Cihlar's poems have appeared in *Blackbird, The South Dakota Review, Green Mountains Review, Crab Creek Review,* and *Southern Humanities Review.* She has been twice nominated for a Pushcart Prize. Her chapbook, "The Insomniac's House," is available from *Dancing Girl Press* and a second chapbook, "This is How She Fails," is available from *Crisis Chronicles Press.* She lives in rural southern Wisconsin.

Acknowledgements

A Double Life in Twenty-Nine Days, Twelve Hours, and Forty-Four Minutes—*Bluestem Magazine*

Coffee Klatch—*The Prose-Poem Project*

Blood Rite—*The Writing Disorder*

Moult—*Architrave Press*

Spiral—*The Nervous Breakdown*

Skunk Stroll—*R. KV. R. Y.*

The Optimist Does Origami—*Pirene's Fountain*

The Muralist—*In Posse Review*

Small Scale Poultry Keeping—*Star*Line*

A Brief Encounter—*The Linnet's Wings*

The Dairy Farmer Told Me His Cows Were Coming into Season—*Corium*

Desire Doesn't Work Here—*In Posse Review*

These Days I Go by the Name Compass—*The Fiddleback Magazine*

www.ingramcontent.com/pod-product-compliance
Lightning Source LLC
Chambersburg PA
CBHW051742040426
42447CB00008B/1268